STEP-BY-STEP COOKING for kids

Recipes from around the world

Marshall Cavendish
Cuisine

Published by Marshall Cavendish Cuisine
An imprint of Marshall Cavendish International
1 New Industrial Road, Singapore 536196

Other Marshall Cavendish Offices:

Marshall Cavendish International. PO Box 65829 London EC1P 1NY, UK • Marshall Cavendish
Corporation. 99 White Plains Road, Tarrytown NY 10591-9001, USA • Marshall Cavendish International
(Thailand) Co Ltd. 253 Asoke, 12th Flr, Sukhumvit 21 Road, Klongtoey Nua, Wattana, Bangkok 10110,
Thailand • Marshall Cavendish (Malaysia) Sdn Bhd, Times Subang, Lot 46, Subang Hi-Tech Industrial
Park, Batu Tiga, 40000 Shah Alam, Selangor Darul Ehsan, Malaysia

Marshall Cavendish is a trademark of Times Publishing Limited

National Library Board Singapore Cataloguing in Publication Data

Step-by-step cooking for kids : recipes from around the world. – Singapore : Marshall Cavendish Cuisine,
c2011.
p. cm.
Includes index.
ISBN : 978-981-4346-41-2

1. International cooking – Juvenile literature.

TX652.5
641.5123 -- dc22   OCN704511206

Printed in Singapore by KWF Printing Pte Ltd

CONTENTS

Introduction   4

Recipes

Peach Licuado Argentina   6

Anzac Biscuits Australia   8

Cocada Branca Brazil   10

Pancakes with Maple
Syrup Canada   12

Leche Con Plátano Chile   14

Tang Yuan China   16

Ensalada de Frutas
Costa Rica   18

Bramborák Czech Republic   20

Grandma's Nut Cake
Egypt   22

Scones England   24

Dabo Kolo Ethiopia   26

Shrove Tuesday Buns
Finland   28

Bûche de Noël France   30

Kinderglüwein Germany   32

Koulourakia Greece   34

Blancmange Haiti   36

Burfi India   38

Fried Tempeh Indonesia   40

Shamrock Cookies Ireland   42

Hamantaschen Israel   44

Pizza Italy   46

Pineapple Fool Jamaica   48

Onigiri Japan   50

Rice Pancakes Kenya   52

Milkshake Madagascar   54

Guacamole Mexico   56

Banch Mongolia   58

Sugar Hearts Netherlands   60

Kiwi-Mango Sorbet
New Zealand   62

Ginger Beer Nigeria   64

Natilla Peru   66

Halo Halo Philippines   68

Nut Mazurek Poland   70

Besitos de Coco
Puerto Rico   72

Russian Sweet Treats
Russia   74

Khoshaf Saudi Arabia   76

Scottish Shortbread
Scotland   78

Sosaties South Africa   80

Kkaegangjong South Korea   82

Crema Frita Spain   84

Coconut Chocolate Balls
Sweden   86

Swiss Fondue Switzerland   88

Watermelon Slushies
Thailand   90

Callaloo Trinidad   92

Pumpkin Dessert Turkey   94

Strawberry Kysil Ukraine   96

Pumpkin Pie United States   98

Sticky Rice with Mango
Vietnam   100

Index   102

INTRODUCTION

Go on a culinary journey around the world as you learn how to cook dishes from 48 countries. In this book, you will discover the favourite dishes of countries such as Argentina, Canada, Ethiopia, the Netherlands, South Korea and many more! With clear step-by-step photographs to guide you along to creating delicious snacks, desserts and main dishes, learning about world cuisine is more fun than ever.

Whether it is sweet treats such as *blancmange* from Haiti and *tang yuan* from China or savoury snacks such as *guacamole* from Mexico and *sosaties* from South Africa, you will have fun cooking up a storm whether it is to share with loved ones or to enjoy yourself.

What's more, you will also learn about the culture, geography and history of the countries as you discover the different cuisines of the world. Each recipe comes with interesting trivia about what makes the country special as well as a map of where the country is located in the world. With this cookbook, getting to know more about the different dishes of the world is both fun and fascinating!

NOTE

Before you start cooking always ask an adult to help you in the kitchen. When using a stove or oven, ask your adult assistant to help. Have an adult to assemble electrical equipment and operate it and always have an adult to help you pour out hot liquids.

Argentina

PEACH LICUADO

Argentina occupies most of the southern half of the South American continent. The country is very large, so its climate and landscape are very different from region to region, with deserts in the northwest and massive glaciers in the south.

Argentine children enjoy a beverage made with fruit, called a *licuado* [lee-CWAH-doh], more than any other drink. Favourite *licuado* flavours are peach and banana.

You will need:

1. Blender
2. Cutting board
3. Measuring cup
4. Knife
5. Spoon
6. Measuring spoons
7. 2 tablespoons sugar
8. 3 ripe peaches
9. 2 cups (480 ml) cold water

3 & 9

1

7

2

8

4

5

6

1 Have an adult help you peel the peaches with the knife. Cut the peaches into small pieces.

2 Spoon the pieces of peach into the blender.

3 Add the sugar and the cold water and blend until smooth. Pour the drink into a glass and add ice. Now you can enjoy a refreshing glass of Argentinian peach *licuado*!

ANZAC BISCUITS

Australia

Australia is a continent in the Southern Hemisphere and includes Tasmania, a smaller island that lies south of the mainland. Due to its location, Australia is often known as "the land down under", particularly by people in the Northern Hemisphere.

During World War I, ANZAC troops made biscuits from ingredients they had available to them and Anzac biscuits became a favourite snack. Australian soldiers received packages of these biscuits from their families. The biscuits can be kept for a long time because they do not contain any milk or eggs. They are quick and simple to make. To vary the taste, add other ingredients such as fruit or nuts.

You will need:
1. Measuring spoons
2. Measuring cup
3. Spoon
4. Wooden spoon
5. Saucepan
6. Nonstick cookie sheet or baking pan
7. Mixing bowl
8. 4 tablespoons butter
9. 1 teaspoon baking soda
10. 2 tablespoons corn syrup
11. 1 cup (115 g) plain flour
12. 1 cup (115 g) rolled oats
13. 2 tablespoons sugar

1 In a bowl, mix together the flour, rolled oats and sugar.

2 Melt the butter in a saucepan over low heat. Stir in corn syrup and baking soda.

3 Add the butter mixture to the dry ingredients in the bowl and mix well.

4 Drop the mixture by teaspoonfuls onto the cookie sheet and flatten them. Bake the biscuits for 10 to 15 minutes at 180°C (350°F). Invite your friends to try them!

Brazil

COCADA BRANCA

Brazil is the largest country in Latin America. In fact, it covers almost half of the continent of South America. The main feature of the country is the Amazon River. The Amazon River is the second longest river in the world after the Nile River in Africa.

Cocada branca is a very sweet Brazilian dessert that tastes especially delicious when served with fruit such as oranges and pineapple. The coconut in the recipe gives the dish a very tropical flavour.

You will need:

1. Wooden spoon
2. Saucepan
3. Measuring cups
4. 1½ cups (180 g) grated coconut
5. ¾ cup (170 g) brown sugar
6. 1 cup (240 ml) milk
7. 4 cloves

1 Bring the sugar, cloves and milk to a boil in the saucepan.

2 Remove the saucepan from the heat and add the grated coconut. Mix well.

3 Cook on low heat for 10 minutes. Chill in the refrigerator overnight and then dig in the next day for a treat you won't forget!

PANCAKES WITH MAPLE SYRUP

Canada

Canada is a huge country stretching from northern United States all the way to the Arctic Ocean and from the island of Newfoundland all the way to Vancouver Island in the Pacific Ocean. Canada is divided into 10 provinces and two territories. Ottawa is the capital of Canada.

Pancakes are very popular for breakfast in Canada. They are often eaten with eggs, bacon or sausages—and, of course, lots of maple syrup!

You will need:

1. 2 mixing bowls
2. Wooden spoon
3. Measuring cups
4. Measuring spoons
5. Whisk
6. Spatula
7. Frying pan
8. 2 eggs
9. 2 cups (480 ml) buttermilk (or sour milk)
10. 1 teaspoon baking soda
11. 2 cups (230 g) plain flour, sifted
12. 2 teaspoons baking powder
13. ½ teaspoon salt
14. 6 tablespoons butter or margarine
15. A bottle or tin of real maple syrup

1 Break the eggs into a large mixing bowl and beat them well. Add the buttermilk and mix it all together.

2 Put the other ingredients (except the butter and syrup) into another bowl and mix them together.

3 Add the dry ingredients to the egg and buttermilk mixture and beat it until it is smooth.

4 Have an adult help you melt 2 tablespoons of the butter in a large frying pan over medium heat. Pour the batter into the frying pan, making it into a circle. Cook the pancake until bubbles start to form. Take a spatula and turn the pancakes over. Cook for 2 more minutes. Remove the pancake to a serving plate, continue until you have used up all of the batter.

5 Put 2 or 3 pancakes on each plate and pour the maple syrup over the top. Pancakes are great for breakfast, but you can eat them at any time of the day!

LECHE CON PLÁTANO

Chile

Chile is located in South America. It is bordered by the Pacific Ocean to the west and the Andes mountain range to the east. Easter Island, the Juan Fernández Archipelago and a section of Antarctica are also part of Chile.

Beginning with Fiestas Patrias and continuing all through summer, Chileans enjoy a drink called *leche con plátano*. This means milk with bananas. Celebrate your summer fiestas by whipping up a batch of *leche con plátano* to help cool you down!

You will need:
1. Measuring spoons
2. Measuring cup
3. Blender
4. Plate
5. 1 cup (240 ml) very cold milk
6. 1 tablespoon sugar
7. 1 small banana

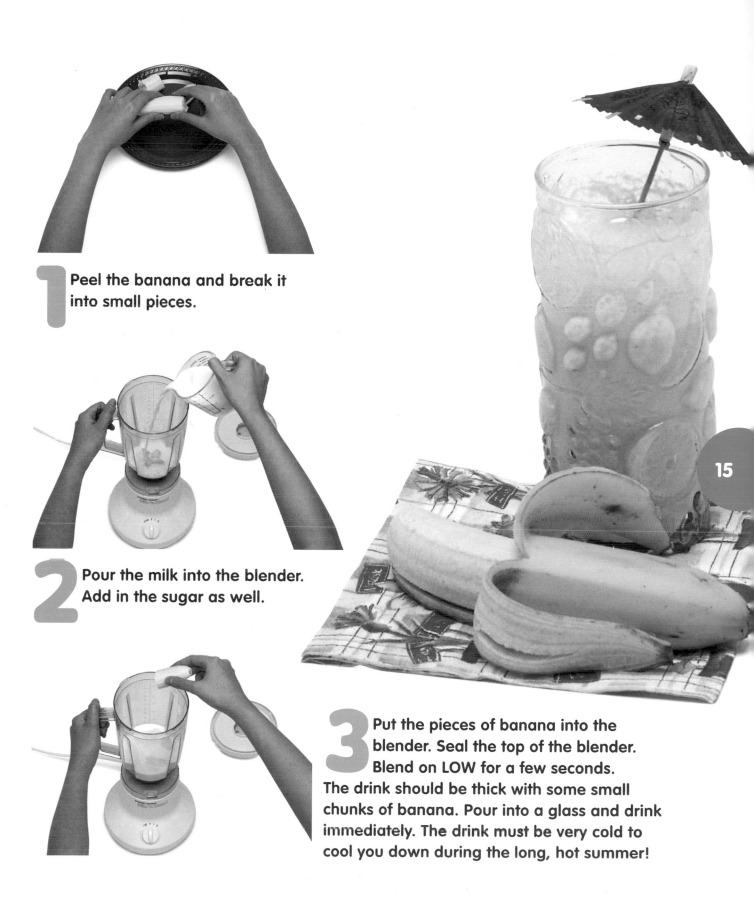

1 Peel the banana and break it into small pieces.

2 Pour the milk into the blender. Add in the sugar as well.

3 Put the pieces of banana into the blender. Seal the top of the blender. Blend on LOW for a few seconds. The drink should be thick with some small chunks of banana. Pour into a glass and drink immediately. The drink must be very cold to cool you down during the long, hot summer!

China

TANG YUAN

China lies in the middle of Asia, between India in the west and Korea and Japan in the east. The soil is rich in the eastern part and farming is one of the most important activities there. The southwest is covered with high mountains and there are many deserts in the north.

Tang yuan is a sweet dessert that is eaten at the Winter Solstice Festival. It is also offered to ancestors as a symbol of family reunion.

You will need:

1. Ladle
2. Wooden spoon
3. Measuring cup
4. Saucepan
5. Large bowl
6. 2 cups (230 g) rice flour
7. 3 cups (690 g) brown sugar
8. 6 cups (1.5 litres) water
9. Red, green and yellow food colouring

1 Mix 1 cup water and the flour together in a bowl.

2 With clean hands, pick up the dough and knead it for a few minutes.

3 Mix the sugar into 5 cups of water in a saucepan. Ask your adult helper to heat the sugar water over medium-high heat.

4 Divide the dough into 3 lumps. Add a different colour to each, working it in until the dough is coloured all the way through. Make sure you wash your hands before switching lumps!

5 Roll the dough into balls the size of large marbles. Then drop them into the sugar water. Ask an adult to help you cook them until they rise to the top. Serve the balls in the syrup. You can eat them hot or cold.

ENSALADA DE FRUTAS

Costa Rica

Costa Rica is a small, beautiful country on the isthmus of Central America. It connects Panama and Nicaragua and is sandwiched between the Pacific Ocean and the Caribbean Sea. Costa Rica is best known for its tropical rain forests and its numerous plant and animal species.

A wide variety of fresh fruit grow in Costa Rica. The Costa Ricans enjoy fruit in juices, salads and desserts. Follow the simple steps below to make *ensalada de frutas* [EN-sah-LAH-dah day FREW-tahs] or fruit salad.

You will need:

1. Spoon
2. Mixing bowl
3. 1 cup (240 ml) warm water
4. 90 g package jello powder
5. 2½ cups (450 g) vanilla ice cream
6. 1 cup (225 g) sliced kiwi fruit
7. 1 cup (225 g) sliced pineapple
8. 1 cup (225 g) sliced strawberries

1 In a mixing bowl, combine the jello powder with warm water. Put the mixture in the refrigerator to cool. Prepare the jello at least one day ahead.

2 Put spoonfuls of sliced kiwi fruit, pineapple and strawberries into a dessert bowl.

3 Add spoonfuls of solidified jello and mix it with the fruit.

4 Put a scoop of ice cream on top of the fruit and jello mixture. Your *ensalada de frutas* is ready to be served!

Czech Republic

BRAMBORÁK

The Czech Republic is a small country in the heart of Europe. It consists of Bohemia in the west, Moravia in the east and Silesia in the northeast. Mountains occupy much of the country, so people sometimes call the Czech Republic "the roof of Europe", because many of Europe's rivers start flowing from the mountains there.

A favourite snack in the Czech Republic is *bramborák* (BRAHM-bo-rahk) or potato pancake. Czechs enjoy eating them at festival time and at family gatherings.

You will need:

1. Frying pan
2. Pot holder
3. Mixing bowl
4. Wooden spoon
5. Pancake turner
6. Measuring spoons
7. ¼ cup (30 g) plain flour
8. ½ teaspoon salt
9. ½ teaspoon pepper
10. 1 egg
11. 1 clove garlic, crushed
12. ½ teaspoon majoram
13. 2 tablespoons milk
14. 2 tablespoons cooking oil
15. 2 cups (450 g) grated potatoes

1 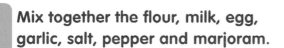 Mix together the flour, milk, egg, garlic, salt, pepper and marjoram.

2 Add the potatoes to this mixture and blend thoroughly.

3 Form patties with the mixture. Then, ask an adult to help you fry them with cooking oil in the frying pan. When the patties are brown, serve and eat!

GRANDMA'S NUT CAKE

Egypt is located in the northeast corner of Africa. Most of Egypt is covered by the Western Desert, which is part of the Sahara. The Nile River cuts through Egypt, flowing from its source in tropical Africa to the Mediterranean Sea.

Egyptians make special sweet treats for Id al-Fitr, an Islamic holiday marking the end of the fasting month. Here is one you could try at home with the help from an adult.

1
2 & 18
11
13
17
3
14
15
19
10
4
16
6 & 12
5
7, 8 & 9

You will need:

1. Wooden spoon
2. Measuring cup
3. Measuring cups
4. Saucepan
5. Measuring spoons
6. Mixing bowls
7. Sieve
8. Baking pan
9. Pot holder
10. ½ cup (113 g) butter
11. 2 cups (460 g) sugar
12. 6 eggs
13. 1½ cups (340 g) plain flour, sifted
14. 3 teaspoons baking powder
15. 1 teaspoon ground cinnamon
16. ½ teaspoon salt
17. 1 cup (250 g) chopped nuts
18. 1 cup (240 ml) water
19. A pinch of fenugreek

1 Mix the butter and 1½ cups sugar. Add the eggs one at a time, beating the mixture.

2 In another bowl, sift together the flour, baking powder, cinnamon and salt. Add the eggs to the flour mixture and mix well. Add the nuts.

3 Pour into a baking pan. It should be about 2.5 cm (1 in) deep. Bake at 180°C (350°F) for 35 minutes. Ask an adult to help you with this part.

4 Combine the rest of the sugar, water and fenugreek in a saucepan. Have an adult help you cook it over low heat, stirring constantly, until the sugar dissolves. Then boil it for 3 minutes. Pour the syrup over the cake before serving.

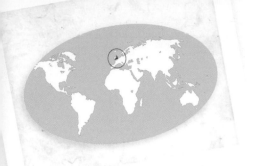

England

SCONES

 England is part of the island of Great Britain in western Europe. The country is famous for its green countryside, but most English people live in big cities. The capital is London.

English people enjoy scones as an afternoon snack, often with a cup of tea. Scones are delicious with jam and whipped cream or just plain butter. They're best when they're freshly baked and still warm.

You will need:

1. Mixing bowl
2. Sieve
3. Wooden spoon
4. Measuring cups
5. Cutting board
6. Rolling pin
7. Cookie cutter
8. Baking tray
9. Wire rack
10. Pot holders
11. Measuring spoons
12. 2½ cups (287 g) self-raising flour
13. ⅓ cup (76 g) butter, cut into small pieces
14. ⅓ cup (69 g) sugar
15. 4 tablespoons milk
16. A pinch of salt
17. Extra flour

1 Wash your hands, then sift the flour and salt into a mixing bowl to get rid of any lumps. Rub the butter into the flour with your fingertips until the mixture is like bread crumbs.

2 Add the sugar and milk and gently squeeze the mixture into a ball using your fingers.

3 Roll the mixture out onto a floured board until it is about 2 cm (¾ in) thick.

4 Cut circles out of the mixture with a cookie cutter. Put them onto a greased baking tray. With an adult's help, bake your scones at 220°C (425°F) for about 10 minutes or until brown on top. Leave them to cool on a rack.

Ethiopia

DABO KOLO

Ethiopia is a landlocked country bordered by Kenya, Somalia, Djibouti, Eritrea and Sudan. Ethiopia is often called the "roof of Africa" because most of the country lies on a very high plateau.

Ethiopians love to feast and after a big meal, they love to eat sweets. *Dabo kolo* is a spicy cookie that is a favourite among Ethiopian kids.

You will need:
1. Spoon
2. Wooden spoon
3. Measuring spoons
4. Measuring cup
5. Cutting board
6. Small bowl
7. Mixing bowl
8. Baking pan
9. Pot holder
10. 3 tablespoons cayenne pepper
11. ½ teaspoon salt
12. ¼ teaspoon ground cloves
13. 1 teaspoon ground ginger
14. ½ teaspoon ground cinnamon
15. 2 tablespoons light oil
16. 1 cup (115 g) whole wheat flour
17. 2 teaspoons sugar
18. ½ cup (120 ml) water

1 Preheat the oven to 177°C (350°F). Combine the flour, sugar and salt in the mixing bowl. In the small bowl, mix the cayenne pepper, cloves, ginger and cinnamon. Add the spices to the flour mixture. Slowly stir in the water.

2 When the mixture turns into a thick paste, knead it on a floured cutting board until it is stiff.

3 Make a well in the centre of the dough and pour in the oil. Fold the dough over the oil and knead it for about 5 minutes.

4 Break off chunks of dough and roll them into 1 cm (1/2 in)-long pieces. Bake for 20 to 30 minutes, until the cookies are brown and crisp. Enjoy!

SHROVE TUESDAY BUNS

Finland is the twelfth largest country in Europe. However, it has one of Europe's smallest populations. Finland's neighbours are Sweden to the west, Norway to the north and Russia to the east.

Eating Shrove Tuesday buns before Easter is a tradition. Some Finns eat the special buns as a dessert in hot milk. Others cut the bun in half, fill the bottom slice with whipped cream and put the top back again. Whichever way you eat it, the bun is delicious.

You will need:

1. Measuring spoons
2. Wooden spoon
3. Measuring cup
4. Whisk
5. Rolling pin
6. Pot holder
7. Wooden board
8. Pastry brush
9. Butter knife
10. Nonstick baking tray
11. Mixing bowl
12. ½ cup (113 g) butter
13. ½ cup (115 g) sugar
14. ⅔ cup (160 ml) lukewarm milk
15. ½ tablespoon crushed cardamom
16. ¼ cup (50 g) dried instant yeast
17. 3 cups (345 g) plain flour
18. Whipped cream
19. 2 eggs
20. 1 teaspoon salt

1 Dissolve the yeast in the milk. Add in 1 beaten egg. Put in the salt, sugar, cardamom and flour and whisk.

3 Using the rolling pin, flatten the dough into a sheet about 1.2 cm (½ in) thick.

2 Add in butter. Knead the dough with your fingers until it does not stick to the sides of the bowl. Leave the dough alone for 30 minutes at room temperature.

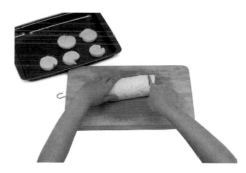

4 Spread butter on the dough, then roll it up.

5 Cut the rolled dough into round pieces and put them on the baking tray. Leave them to rise for about an hour. Break the other egg and beat it. Brush the top of the buns with the egg and bake them at 225°C (440°F) for about 10 minutes. When they have cooled down, cut the buns in half and spread whipped cream over the bottom half. Put the top half back on and your buns are ready!

France

BÛCHE DE NOËL

France is one of the oldest nations in Europe. It lies near the edge of the continent and has a long coastline on the Atlantic Ocean. The capital is Paris.

Bûche de Noël means Yule log or Christmas log. It is made with chocolate cake and ice cream and makes a delicious Christmas treat. Here's the recipe so you can make your own Christmas surprise.

You will need:
1. Mixing bowl
2. Baking tray or pan
3. Wooden spoon
4. Butter knife
5. Spoon
6. Measuring cup
7. Cutting board
8. Pot holder
9. ½ box chocolate cake mix
10. 4 cups (1 litre) vanilla ice cream
11. 1 egg
12. ½ cup (120 ml) milk
13. Chocolate frosting

1 With clean hands, mix the egg and milk with the cake mix or follow the instructions on the back of the box of cake mix.

2 Pour the mixture into a baking tray. With an adult's help, cook the cake according to the instructions on the box.

3 Let the cake cool, then spread the ice cream evenly over the cake.

4 Carefully roll the cake.

5 With a butter knife, frost the cake so that it looks like a log and decorate it with holly or other Christmas decorations.

Germany

KINDERGLÜWEIN

Germany is right in the middle of Europe. It is surrounded by 11 other countries. Hardly any other country has as many neighbours. Most of the country is covered by mountains and forests, but in the north the land is flat.

Kinderglüwein [KIN-der-GLUE-vine] is a very popular cold weather drink in Germany. This cider is often prepared at home during the Christmas season. It may be served with German Christmas cookies, cakes and grilled sausages. It not only tastes good, it is healthy too.

You will need:
1. Measuring spoons
2. Saucepan
3. Knife
4. Wooden spoon
5. Ladle
6. Cutting board
7. 4 cups (1 litre) grape juice, cherry juice or apple juice
8. 4 whole cloves
9. 2 cinnamon sticks
10. 1 tablespoon lemon juice
11. A pinch of cardamom
12. ½ an apple, thinly sliced, with an adult's help

1 Pour the juice into the saucepan.

2 Add the spices and lemon juice.

3 Have an adult help you turn on the burner under the pan. Put in the apple slices and turn down the heat.

4 Let the drink simmer at a low heat for 5 to 10 minutes. The longer it cooks, the stronger the flavour.

5 Take the saucepan off the stove and pour the drink into cups using a ladle. Drink while it is still warm. *Prost!*—that's German for "Cheers!"

Greece

KOULOURAKIA

Greece is a very old part of Europe and is more than 4,000 years old. It is a small country with over 1,400 islands that dot the blue waters around the Greek mainland. The capital of Greece is Athens, named after Athena, the goddess of wisdom.

Bread is a very important item in the Greek menu and is served at every meal. Many Greek Orthodox festivals are celebrated with special breads. One of the most popular breads is *koulourakia* [kou-lou-RA-kia], a sweet roll you can make yourself!

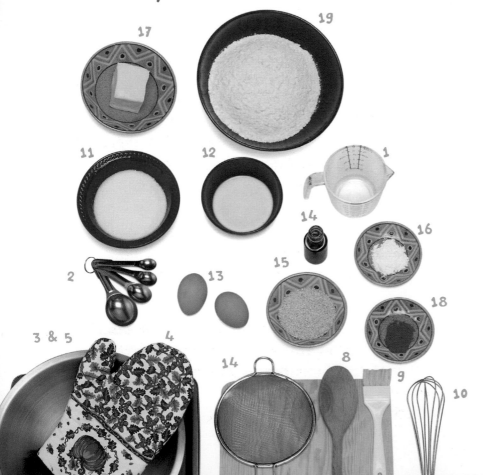

You will need:
1. Measuring cup
2. Measuring spoons
3. Mixing bowl
4. Pot holder
5. Nonstick baking tray
6. Sieve
7. Cutting board
8. Wooden spoon
9. Brush
10. Whisk
11. ¾ cup (150 g) powdered sugar
12. 2 tablespoons milk
13. 2 eggs
14. ½ teaspoon vanilla extract
15. ¼ cup (50 g) white sesame seeds
16. 1½ teaspoons baking powder
17. ½ cup (113 g) butter
18. ¼ teaspoon ground cinammon
19. 2½ cups (290 g) plain flour

1 Whisk the butter, sugar, milk and vanilla extract together until the mixture is light and fluffy. Beat the eggs and add three-quarters of it into the mixture, whisking well.

2 Sift the flour, ground cinammon and baking powder into the mixture.

3 Stir the mixture until a soft dough is formed. Knead the dough a little. Shape the dough into pencil-like shapes and make rings, figure-eights or coils.

4 Place the shapes on a nonstick baking tray. Brush the remaining egg over the shapes and sprinkle sesame seeds over them.

5 Get an adult to help you bake the biscuits in a moderate oven at 190°C (375°F) for 15 to 20 minutes or until they are golden brown. Now you have delicious *koulourakia* for a mouthwatering snack!

Haiti

BLANCMANGE

Haiti is located on the western side of the island of Hispaniola in the West Indies. This former French colony was the second country in the world, after the United States, to declare its independence.

Haitians have a sweet tooth, so they love *blancmange* [blahn-MAHNGE]. Richly flavoured with coconut, this light dessert is a favourite of both adults and children.

You will need:
1. Bowl
2. Saucepan
3. Wooden spoon
4. Measuring cup
5. Measuring spoons
6. Pot holder
7. Nonstick baking sheet
8. 1½ cups (360 ml) coconut cream
9. 1½ cups (360 ml) evaporated milk
10. 1½ cups (360 ml) sweetened condensed milk
11. 1 tablespoon unflavoured gelatin
12. ½ cup (114 g) grated coconut
13. 1 tablespoon sugar

1 Pour 1 cup water into the saucepan. Heat the water and dissolve the gelatin in it. Add the coconut cream, evaporated milk and condensed milk. Bring the mixture to a boil over moderate heat, stirring constantly.

2 Remove the saucepan from the heat and immediately pour the mixture into a bowl. Let it cool at room temperature, then refrigerate it for at least four 4 hours.

3 Preheat the oven to broil. Cover the bottom of a nonstick baking sheet with grated coconut and sprinkle sugar over them. Place the baking sheet under the broiler for 5 to 10 minutes until the grated coconut is golden brown. Remove the baking sheet from the oven and let the coconut cool.

4 Just before serving, top the blancmange with the toasted coconut.

India

BURFI

India is a huge country and more crowded than almost anywhere else in the world. One person in every six people on Earth lives in India. At the heart of India are the Indus and Ganges rivers, which bring life to the plains around them. The Ganges is sacred to Indians.

Here is a recipe for a simple Indian treat called *burfi*. Try making it for Diwali, the Indian festival of lights. There are many kinds of *burfi* made with different kinds of nuts and flours.

You will need:
1. Pastry brush
2. Measuring spoons
3. Small saucepan
4. Frying pan
5. Baking tray
6. Wooden spoon
7. Knife
8. Blender
9. 2 cups (500 g) raw cashews
10. 1 cup (240 ml) sweetened condensed milk
11. Butter for greasing tray
12. 1 teaspoon plain flour

1 Ask an adult to help you put the cashews in a frying pan and cook them over low heat. Stir them constantly until they are golden brown. Be careful not to burn them!

2 Grind the roasted cashews. You can use a blender or crush them in a bag with a rolling pin.

3 Mix half the ground cashews, the condensed milk and the flour in a saucepan. With an adult, cook the mixture for a few minutes until it is almost solid.

4 Grease the baking tray with the butter. Press the cashew mixture into the greased pan. Pour the remaining cashews over the top and press them into the mixture. Let it cool and then cut the *burfi* into squares.

Indonesia

FRIED TEMPEH

Indonesia is the largest archipelago in the world. It is composed of five main islands—Sumatra, Java, Kalimantan, Sulawesi and Irian Jaya—and 13,000 smaller islands. Its territory lies across the equator, so the weather is hot and humid all year long.

Tempeh is an Indonesian speciality of fermented soy beans that are pressed into a cake. After you fry it, it tastes like meat.

You will need:
1. Frying pan
2. Cutting board
3. Knife
4. Fork
5. Measuring spoons
6. 1 package *tempeh*
7. 1 clove garlic
8. ½ teaspoon ground coriander
9. 1 tablespoon light soy sauce
10. 6 tablespoons butter

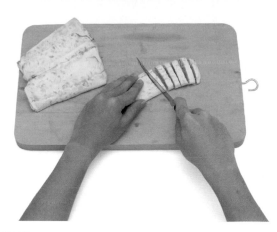

1 Slice the *tempeh* into 0.5 cm (¹/₄ in) slices. (The *tempeh* we used here is the way it looks in Indonesia—yours may look a little different.)

2 Chop the garlic into very small bits (or use a garlic press).

3 Melt the butter in a frying pan. Add the garlic and coriander and fry until golden (about 1 minute).

4 Add the tempeh. Dribble soy sauce over the tempeh and fry until browned. Use the fork to turn them over and fry the other side. Serve with some rice.

Ireland

SHAMROCK COOKIES

Ireland is divided in two parts: Northern Ireland, which has ties with England and the Republic of Ireland. Rain from the Atlantic Ocean blows across the island, making it green both in summer and winter. For this reason, Ireland is often called the Emerald Isle.

The Irish people grow lots of potatoes and many Irish recipes include them. These cookies will help you and your family celebrate Saint Patrick's Day.

You will need:
1. Large bowl
2. Wooden spoon
3. Measuring spoons
4. Measuring cups
5. Sieve
6. Pot holder
7. Pastry brush
8. Baking tray
9. Spoon
10. Potato masher
11. 1¼ cups (300 g) hot, cooked potatoes
12. ½ cup (115 g) sugar
13. ¼ cup (60 ml) honey
14. 1 cup (227 g) butter or margarine
15. 1 cup (115 g) plain flour
16. 2 teaspoons baking powder
17. 1 teaspoon ground cinnamon or ground allspice
18. ¼ teaspoon ground cloves
19. ½ teaspoon grated nutmeg
20. ½ teaspoon salt
21. 1 egg for brushing
22. Green sprinkles for decorating

1 Place the hot, cooked potatoes in a large bowl and mash them thoroughly.

2 Cream the sugar, syrup and butter together. Beat in the mashed potatoes.

3 Sift together the flour, baking powder, spices and salt. Add sifted, dry ingredients to the batter to make dough. Mix until it is smooth.

4 Using a teaspoon, drop 3 small mounds of dough close together to form the shape of a shamrock on a lightly greased cookie sheet.

5 Brush the tops of the cookies with some lightly beaten egg. Top with green sprinkles and bake for 20 minutes at 190°C (375°F). This recipe makes 40 cookies or more, so you can invite your friends over to share them.

HAMANTASCHEN

Israel is part of the region known as the Middle East, which lies between North Africa and Asia. People have lived there for at least 100,000 years. Many of the events in the Bible took place in the land we now call Israel. The capital of Israel is Jerusalem. Jerusalem is a holy city for Christians, Muslims and Jews.

Hamantaschen means "Haman's pockets." Enjoy making a version of *hamantaschen* with an adult helper.

You will need:

1. Wooden spoon
2. Spatula
3. Baking tray
4. Pot holder
5. Measuring cups
6. Measuring spoons
7. ½ cup (70 g) plain flour, sifted
8. 2 teaspoons baking powder
9. 1 cup (230 g) sugar
10. 1 cup (227 g) butter
11. ¾ cup (150 g) chocolate chips
12. 2 eggs
13. 1 teaspoon vanilla extract

1 Wash your hands, then mix the flour and baking powder together in a bowl.

2 Mash the butter into small pieces until the mixture is smooth.

3 Beat the eggs and add them and the vanilla to the flour mixture.

4 When the mixture is smooth, drop a small amount onto a greased baking tray and top with a few chocolate chips. You can also make the cookies into a triangle shape using your fingers. Keep on doing this until you've used all the mixture—about 24 cookies.

5 With an adult's help, bake the cookies in an oven at 180°C (350°F) for 15 to 20 minutes. Be careful around the hot oven—be sure to have an adult help you take the cookies out.

Italy

PIZZA

Italy occupies a peninsula shaped like a boot that juts out from the southern coast of Europe into the Mediterranean Sea. Most of the country is covered with hills or mountains, including the Alps in the north, which are the highest mountains in Europe. It also includes the two large islands of Sicily and Sardinia. Perhaps the most popular food that comes from Italy is pizza. The city of Naples is known to be the birthplace of the popular dish.

You will need:

1. Measuring cups
2. Measuring spoons
3. Mixing bowl
4. Knife
5. Pizza pan or baking sheet
6. Wooden spoon
7. Cutting board
8. Pot holder
9. Sieve
10. 1 cup (115 g) plain flour
11. 1 teaspoon baking powder
12. ¼ teaspoon salt
13. ⅓ cup (80 ml) milk
14. 3 tablespoons salad oil
15. ¼ cup (25 g) grated parmesan cheese
16. 1 cup (115 g) tomato sauce
17. ½ tablespoon chopped onions
18. ¼ teaspoon oregano
19. ⅛ teaspoon pepper
20. 1 cup (115 g) shredded mozzarella cheese
21. ¼ cup (50 g) sliced mushrooms
22. ⅛ cup (25 g) sliced pitted olives

1 Sift flour. Measure flour, baking powder, salt, milk and 2 tablespoons salad oil into bowl. Stir until mixture leaves side of bowl.

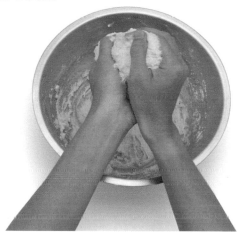

2 Gather dough together and press into a ball. Knead dough 10 times to make it smooth.

3 Press the dough into pizza pan or baking sheet. Turn up edge a little bit all around. Brush with salad oil.

4 Layer pizza toppings in order listed. Bake at 220°C (425°F) for 20 to 25 minutes. Cut into wedges and eat!

Jamaica

PINEAPPLE FOOL

Jamaica is a little tropical island in the Caribbean Sea and some of the world's most beautiful beaches can be found here. Kingston, the capital of Jamaica, is on the southern coast of the island.

A fool is a dessert made of fruit, sugar, cream and sometimes eggs. Here's a really yummy pineapple fool that is simple to make. You can also use fruit like raspberries instead of pineapples.

You will need:
1. Knife
2. Cutting board
3. Sieve
4. Whisk
5. Bowl
6. Measuring spoons
7. Wooden spoon
8. A pineapple
9. ¾ cup (180 ml) cream
10. 2 to 3 tablespoons sugar
11. ½ teaspoon vanilla extract

1 Have an adult help you cut a fresh pineapple into small cubes. Put the cubes in a sieve to drain for at least 10 minutes.

2 Whip the cream in a bowl until it is stiff enough to hold its shape. Add sugar to the cream. Pour in the vanilla extract. Mix well.

3 Chill the whipped cream and pineapple cubes separately in the refrigerator. Just before serving, add the cubes to the cream and blend them together.

4 Spoon your pineapple fool into individual bowls or sundae glasses. Serve right away!

Japan

ONIGIRI

Japan is a small group of islands lying between the Pacific Ocean and the Sea of Japan. There are four main islands in the archipelago: Honshu, Shikoku, Hokkaido and Kyushu. Most people live on the main island, Honshu. The capital of Japan is Tokyo.

A favourite Japanese snack at festival time is *onigiri* [o-NEE-gee-ree]. These delicious and healthy snacks are made from rice. Sometimes the rice is wrapped in seaweed. Other times it is covered with sesame seeds.

You will need:
1. Cutting board
2. Saucepan
3. Wooden spoon
4. Measuring cup
5. Knife
6. Scissors
7. Plate
8. 1 cup (225 g) rice
9. 1¼ cups (300 ml) water
10. 3 sour plums
11. 1 sheet dried seaweed
12. Salt
13. ¼ cup (40 g) white sesame seeds, roasted

1 With an adult's help, put the rice in a saucepan with 1¼ cups water. Bring the water to a boil on high heat and cover the pan. Lower the heat when you see steam coming from the edge of the lid. Simmer rice for 12 to 13 minutes on low heat.

2 While the rice is cooking, ask your adult helper to make a slit in the plums with a knife and remove the pit from inside.

4 Ask your adult helper to cut the seaweed into strips. Now wrap the rice triangle in seaweed or coat with sesame seeds. *Onigiri* is eaten hot or cold with your hands.

3 After the rice has cooled completely, pick up a handful and make a well in the middle. Put a sour plum inside. Put some salt in your hands, then squeeze the rice to make a triangle. Be sure to close up the middle completely so the plum is not showing. Repeat this step with the other 2 plums.

Kenya

RICE PANCAKES

Kenya is located on the eastern coast of Africa. The country gets its name from Mount Kenya, an extinct volcano that was once higher than Mount Everest. Its capital, Nairobi, is one of the largest and most modern cities in Africa.

The Arabs brought rice and spices to Kenya when they arrived on the coast centuries ago. Their influence can be tasted in the food of the Swahilis living on the coast.

You will need:

1. Large bowl
2. Frying pan
3. Measuring cups
4. Spatula
5. Wooden spoon
6. Measuring spoons
7. Dish towel (not terrycloth)
8. 1 teaspoon instant dried yeast
9. ½ to 1 cup (120 to 240 ml) warm water
10. 1 cup (200 g) sugar
11. 2¾ cups (385 g) rice flour
12. ¼ teaspoon ground cardamom
13. ¼ cup (60 ml) canned coconut milk
14. ½ cup (120 ml) vegetable oil

1 Dissolve the yeast in ½ cup warm water. Add a pinch of sugar and set aside in a warm place for 5 minutes. The mixture should foam up.

2 In the bowl, combine sugar, flour and cardamom. Add the coconut milk and the yeast mixture and stir. It should be like pancake batter. If the batter is too thick, add a little water until the batter runs slowly from the spoon.

3 Cover the bowl with a towel and set aside in a warm place for about 1 hour or until the mixture has nearly doubled in volume.

4 Heat 1 tablespoon oil over medium-high heat. Pour ½ cup of batter into the pan and swirl it around to form a pancake. Cook until bubbles form, then turn pancake over and cook the other side. Remove pancake to a serving plate. Repeat with the rest of the batter.

Madagascar

MILKSHAKE

Madagascar is the fourth largest island in the world. Its nearest neighbours are the islands of Réunion and Mauritius to the east and the Comoro Islands and the African country of Mozambique to the west. Madagascar's capital is Antananarivo, meaning "town of a thousand warriors".

The Malagasy use bananas in many dishes such as fritters and flambe. Try this milkshake made with bananas and don't forget to give your milkshake that special Malagasy touch by adding vanilla flavouring and a little coconut.

You will need:
1. Spoon
2. Measuring spoons
3. Blender
4. 2 cups (480 ml) milk
5. 3 tablespoons vanilla ice cream
6. 1 teaspoon vanilla powder or extract
7. 1 teaspoon shredded coconut
8. 1 tablespoon honey
9. 1 large banana, cut into pieces
10. About 15 strawberries

1 Put strawberries, banana pieces, honey and 1 cup milk into the blender. Blend until smooth.

2 Add ice cream to the mixture. Blend just until mixed.

3 Stir in the rest of the milk, vanilla extract and shredded coconut. Chill your milkshake in the refrigerator and you have a refreshing drink.

Mexico

GUACAMOLE

Mexico lies just south of the United States. Many years ago, the western part of the United States also belonged to Mexico, including California, Arizona, New Mexico, Colorado, Nevada and Utah.

A lot of Mexican food is made from different variations of corn, beans and rice. These three ingredients, along with fruits and vegetables, make a healthy diet. Another favourite festival food is *guacamole* [gwah-kah-MOE-lay] made with avocados. You can make *guacamole* easily at home.

You will need:
1. Spoon
2. Fork
3. Bowl
4. Knife
5. Measuring spoons
6. 2 ripe avocados
7. Half a small onion
8. 2 to 3 sprigs fresh coriander leaves
9. 1 jalapeño pepper, if you like it spicy
10. 2 tomatoes
11. 2 tablespoons lemon juice
12. Salt

1 With clean hands, cut the avocados in half, take out the large seeds and scoop out the avocado.

2 Put the avocado in a bowl and mash it up with a fork.

3 With an adult's help, chop up the onion, coriander leaves, jalapeño pepper and tomatoes. Add them all to the avocado.

4 Add the lemon juice and a little salt until it tastes right. Mix it well. Dip in your tortilla chips and enjoy!

Mongolia

BANCH

Mongolia is divided into two countries—Inner Mongolia, which is part of China and Outer Mongolia, which is an independent republic. The country has many lakes and a large desert called the Gobi Desert. Nomads, people who travel from place to place, live on Mongolia's flat grasslands called steppes.

One of the Mongolians' favourite meat dishes is *banch* or steamed lamb dumplings. You can also make this delicious dish with beef, as we have done here.

You will need:
1. Measuring spoons
2. Mixing bowl
3. Cutting board
4. Spoon
5. Wooden spoon
6. Rolling pin
7. 1 cup (230 g) plain flour
8. ³⁄₄ cup (150 ml) cold water
9. 1 teaspoon pepper
10. 1 teaspoon salt
11. 1 cup (230 g) ground beef
12. ³⁄₄ cup (90 g) chopped cabbage
13. ³⁄₄ cup (90 g) chopped onions

1 Mix the beef, onions and cabbage together in the mixing bowl. Add salt and pepper to the mixture.

2 Mix flour and cold water to make a soft dough. Let the dough sit for 10 minutes.

3 Roll small balls of dough into thin circles, each with a diameter of about 7.5 cm (3 in). The dough circles should be thin at the edges and thicker in the middle.

4 Place a tablespoon of the meat and vegetable mixture onto each circle of dough. Fold the edges over the mixture to form a flowerlike pattern. Ask your adult helper to steam the dumplings for 20 minutes. Now you have a pretty Mongolian snack!

Netherlands

SUGAR HEARTS

The Netherlands is a small and densely populated monarchy in northwestern Europe. The country got its name from the fact that most of the country lies below sea level. It is often called Holland as well, although this name actually applies only to the two provinces of North and South Holland.

Sinterklaas is a traditional winter holiday observed in the Netherlands on December the 5th. Sinterklaas, good children and sugar hearts go together!

You will need:
1. Wax paper
2. Wooden spoon
3. Measuring spoons
4. Saucepan
5. Measuring cup
6. 1 or more heart-shaped baking dishes
7. ½ cup (120 ml) milk
8. 2 teaspoons cocoa powder
9. 1 teaspoon butter
10. 1 cup (200 g) sugar

1 Mix the sugar and cocoa in a saucepan. Add milk, stir well and bring to a boil.

2 Let the mixture simmer till it thickens into syrup. Once the syrup is slow to flow from the spoon, remove the syrup from the fire and stir till cloudy.

3 Line the baking dish with wax paper. Pour the syrup into the dish before it hardens.

4 Let the hearts cool off and harden, then carefully lift the sugar heart out of the baking dish. Remove the wax paper and you've got your sugar heart!

New Zealand

KIWI-MANGO SORBET

New Zealand is a group of islands in the southern Pacific Ocean. There are two main islands, North Island and South Island and some other smaller islands. Its closest neighbour is Australia.

New Zealand's most famous fruit is the kiwifruit. It is rich in vitamin C and is used a lot in New Zealand cooking. Follow these simple steps to make a refreshing kiwi treat!

You will need:
1. Blender
2. Square cake pan
3. Spoon
4. Measuring spoons
5. 1 can mango slices
6. 6 kiwifruit, peeled and sliced
7. 1 tablespoon of fresh orange juice

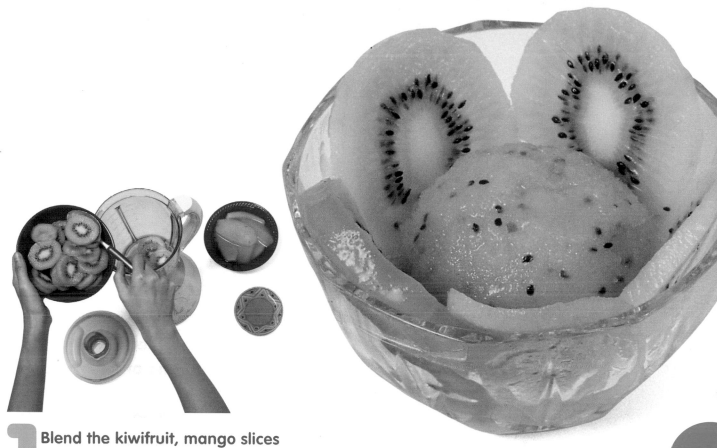

1 Blend the kiwifruit, mango slices (including the syrup in the can) and orange juice to make a puree.

2 Pour the mixture into the cake pan and freeze it for about an hour, until ice crystals start to form.

3 Blend the icy mixture. Then pour it back into the cake pan and freeze it. Place scoops of the frozen sorbet into dessert bowls and serve it with slices of kiwifruit. Now you have a refreshing and cool dessert!

Nigeria

GINGER BEER

Nigeria has the most people of any country in Africa. It faces the Atlantic Ocean, where West Africa and Central Africa meet. The country is named after the Niger River, one of the longest rivers in the world.

On a hot day or during festive occasions, Nigerians like to cool down by drinking ginger beer. The drink is popular at parties and feasts too.

You will need:
1. Measuring spoons
2. Measuring cup
3. Glass
4. Large mixing bowl
5. Sieve
6. Spoon
7. Wooden spoon
8. Saucepan
9. 2½ cups (670 g) fresh chopped ginger
10. 6 cups (1.5 litres) water
11. 2 cups (400 g) sugar
12. Seltzer water
13. Lemon slices
14. Ice cubes

1 Stir the ginger with the water and sugar in a saucepan. Simmer for 30 minutes, stirring occasionally. Let the mixture cool.

2 Strain the mixture.

3 Pour ¼ cup of the mixture into a glass. Fill the glass with seltzer water, a slice of lemon and ice. Stir. This recipe makes 16 refreshing glasses of ginger beer!

Peru

NATILLA

Peru is in South America, south of the equator. There are three types of climate in Peru. Along the coast, it's very hot and dry like a desert. In the Andes Mountains, which run through the middle of Peru, it is much colder than the coast. In the northeast, the weather is hot and wet.

One special treat that Peruvian children really enjoy is *natilla* [nah-TEE-ya] or caramel sauce. They like to put the sauce on bananas and peaches.

You will need:

1. Measuring cups
2. Measuring spoons
3. Big pot
4. Medium-size pot
5. Bowl
6. Wooden spoon
7. Pot holder
8. Knife
9. Cutting board
10. 1 can (360 ml) evaporated milk
11. 2 cups (480 ml) milk
12. ½ teaspoon baking soda
13. 1½ cups (350 g) packed dark brown sugar
14. ¼ cup (60 ml) water
15. 3–4 cups (about 600 g) of your favourite fruit

1 Mix the evaporated milk, regular milk and baking soda together in the big pot. Heat this mixture until it boils, then take it off the stove.

2 Mix the sugar and water in the medium-size pot and heat over low heat. Stir until the sugar melts into the water.

3 Add the sugar to the milk mixture and cook everything together over medium-low heat. Cook until sauce becomes thick and golden brown in color, about 1 hour. Put sauce in a serving bowl, cover and refrigerate for 4 hours.

4 Cut fruit into pieces and cover with sauce. Then enjoy a Peruvian treat!

Philippines

HALO HALO

The islands of the Philippines form the world's second largest archipelago after Indonesia. There are three main island groups: Luzon, the Visayas and Mindanao.

Filipinos love sweet desserts and a particularly easy one to make is *halo halo* [ha-LOW ha-LOW], which means "mix mix". This refreshing sweet treat contains an interesting variety of ingredients. Try it on a hot day to cool down!

You will need:

1. Spoon
2. Measuring spoons
3. Mixing bowl
4. ⅔ cup (160 ml) evaporated milk
5. 2 tablespoons dried coconut flakes
6. 2 tablespoons sugar
7. 2 tablespoons corn kernels
8. 2 tablespoons tapioca
9. 8 tablespoons crushed ice
10. 2 tablespoons cubed sweet potato, steamed until tender
11. 2 tablespoons canned palm fruit
12. 2 tablespoons macademia nuts
13. 1 sliced banana
14. 2 tablespoons frozen custard
15. 2 tablespoons sweetened kidney beans

1 Mix together all ingredients except the evaporated milk, sugar and crushed ice.

2 Put some of this mixture into a serving bowl and add the crushed ice.

3 Add more of the mixture on top of the ice.

4 Add half the sugar and half the evaporated milk to each serving and enjoy a sweet treat.

Poland

NUT MAZUREK

The northern part of Poland is the land of lakes and it is mostly bordered by the Baltic Sea. Central Poland is a flat, wide-stretching plain. Along Poland's southern frontier are the Carpathian and the Sudeten mountains.

The traditional *nut mazurek* cake is the highlight of Easter in Poland, where there is lots of feasting and celebrations to celebrate the resurrection of Christ.

You will need:

1. Large mixing bowl
2. Baking tray
3. Pot holder
4. Butter knife
5. Cutting board
6. Whisk
7. Measuring spoons
8. ½ cup (60 g) whole almonds
9. Chocolate frosting
10. 5 egg whites
11. 6 tablespoons powdered sugar
12. ½ cup (100 g) ground almonds
13. 1 teaspoon flour
14. 2 teaspoons butter

1 Use a whisk to whip the egg whites and the powdered sugar together until they become like a stiff cream.

2 Mix in the ground almonds.

3 Cover the baking tray with a thin layer of butter and sprinkle it with flour. Pour the mixture into the baking tray. Bake at 175°C (350°F) for 35 to 40 minutes.

4 When the *mazurek* base is done, let it cool down. Then, spread a layer of chocolate icing over the top of the cake with a butter knife and decorate it with halved almonds. Your delicious nut *mazurek* cake is ready to be served!

Puerto Rico

BESITOS DE COCO

Puerto Rico is one of the warm, mountainous islands that make up the West Indies. Puerto Rico is the only Spanish colony that never declared its independence, although a few unsuccessful rebellions were attempted. Today, it is a commonwealth of the United States.

These chewy little cookies are called *besitos de coco* [bay-SEE-tohs day KOH-koh], which means coconut kisses. Try them and they'll be sure to make your fiesta extra special!

You will need:
1. Pastry brush
2. Spatula
3. Wooden spoon
4. Measuring spoons
5. Measuring cups
6. Large bowl
7. Baking tray
8. Pot holder
9. 3 cups (225 g) coconut flakes
10. ½ cup (70 g) plain flour
11. 4 egg yolks
12. 1 cup (200 g) brown sugar
13. ¼ teaspoon salt
14. ¼ cup (57 g) butter, softened
15. ½ teaspoon vanilla extract

1 With clean hands, measure all the ingredients into a large bowl and mix them together using the wooden spoon.

2 Pick up a spoonful of the batter and roll it into a ball. Continue until you've used up all the batter. You should have about 24 balls.

3 Grease a baking tray with butter. With an adult's help, preheat the oven to 180°C (350°F).

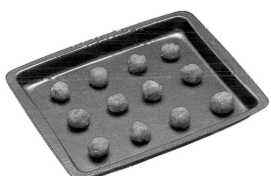

4 Spread the balls out on the greased baking tray. Put them in the oven. Be very careful and be sure to use a pot holder (ask an adult to help you with this). Bake them for 30 to 40 minutes until they're golden brown.

RUSSIAN SWEET TREATS

Russia

Russia is the biggest country in the world. It stretches right across eastern Europe and northern Asia. Russia has many different landscapes—icy deserts, swamps, mountains, plains and pine forests.

Russians enjoy sweet food at many of their festivals. You can make these sweet treats yourself. When you bite into them, you get a sudden taste of the sugar, walnut and cinnamon filling. They're delicious!

You will need:

1. Large mixing bowl
2. Small mixing bowl
3. Measuring cups
4. Measuring spoons
5. Wooden spoon
6. Plate
7. Aluminium foil
8. Rolling pin
9. Cutting board
10. Spoon
11. Knife
12. Baking tray
13. Pot holders
14. ½ cup (113 g) unsalted butter, softened
15. 1 cup (120 g) cream cheese, softened
16. 1 cup (120 g) plain flour
17. ⅛ teaspoon salt
18. ½ cup (60 g) chopped walnuts
19. ¼ cup (30 g) sugar
20. 1 teaspoon cinnamon
21. Extra flour

1 Combine the butter and cream cheese in the large mixing bowl. Stir until completely combined. Add the flour and salt. Mix well.

2 Shape the dough into seven balls. Put them on a dinner plate, cover with aluminium foil and put into the refrigerator for several hours.

3 Lightly dust your cutting board with some flour. Roll the balls into 15 cm (6 in) circles. Cut each circle into quarters.

4 In the small mixing bowl, combine the walnuts, sugar and cinnamon. Drop a rounded teaspoon of this mixture onto each quarter of the dough. To close the cookie, pinch together the edges of the dough to form a triangle. Place the cookies on an ungreased baking tray. Bake at 180°C (350°F) for 15 minutes or until lightly browned. Makes 28 sweet treats.

Saudi Arabia

KHOSHAF

Saudi Arabia occupies 80 per cent of the Arabian Peninsula. Saudi Arabia is an extremely dry country, with much of the land made up of scorching hot rock or sandy desert. Under the rocks and sand lie the biggest oil reserves in the world.

During Ramadan, everyone waits patiently for sunset so they can break the fast with the evening meal. *Khoshaf* [koe-SHAAF], a snack of sweetened fruit, is often served for the evening meal.

You will need:

1. Saucepan
2. Mixing bowl
3. Wooden spoon
4. Spoon
5. Measuring spoons
6. 1 cup (240 ml) water
7. ½ cup (57 g) mixed nuts
8. ¾ cup (114 g) dried prunes
9. ½ cup (57 g) mixed dried fruits
10. 2 dried figs, chopped
11. ¾ cup (85 g) raisins
12. Plain yoghurt
13. ¼ teaspoon ground nutmeg
14. 2 cinnamon sticks
15. 1 cup (227 g) dried apricots
16. 2 tablespoons sugar

1 Put all the fruit in the mixing bowl. Add water until the fruit is covered and let the fruit soak overnight.

2 Have your adult helper help you bring 1 cup of water and the sugar to a boil in the saucepan. Boil 15 to 20 minutes, stirring constantly until the mixture thickens into a syrup.

3 Add the soaked fruit, nuts and spices to the syrup. Stir well, let the mixture cool and refrigerate.

4 Remove cinnamon sticks and serve the chilled *khoshaf* in glass bowls. Top each serving with a spoonful of yoghurt. Enjoy!

SCOTTISH SHORTBREAD

Scotland

Scotland is one of four countries that make up the United Kingdom. The others are England, Northern Ireland and Wales. It has nearly 800 islands off its rugged coastline. The capital city of Scotland is Edinburgh [ed-in-BRUH].

The Scots are famous for their shortbread, a crisp, buttery, rich biscuit eaten as a snack with tea or after dinner. Shortbread is traditionally served broken into bite-size pieces.

You will need:
1. Electric mixer
2. Pot holder
3. Mixing bowl
4. Measuring cup
5. Baking pan
6. Cutting board
7. Wooden spoon
8. Fork
9. $\frac{1}{2}$ cup (60 g) ground rice flour
10. 1 cup (230 g) butter
11. 1 cup (115 g) plain flour
12. $\frac{1}{2}$ cup (60 g) sugar

1 Have an adult help you preheat the oven to 180°C (350°F). Cream the butter with the electric mixer until it starts to take on a pale appearance. Gradually add sugar, beating the mixture until it is light and fluffy.

2 Slowly add the flour to the mixture and knead for about 5 minutes to form a stiff dough.

3 Spread the dough in the baking pan. Flatten it with the heel of your hand until it evenly covers the bottom.

4 Use a knife to cut the dough into 8 wedges. Use the fork to prick the surface of the dough at regular intervals, so the shortbread will be crispy. Ask an adult to place the dough in the oven for 8 to 10 minutes. Then reduce the heat to 150°C (300°F) and bake for another 10 to 15 minutes until the shortbread is crisp and golden. Cool before serving and you have a delicious Scottish treat!

South Africa

SOSATIES

Covering the southern tip of the African continent, South Africa has a countryside as mixed as its people. In the almost tropical northeast lies the Kruger National Park, one of the world's largest wildlife reserves.

Sosaties are skewered meat grilled over a fire in what South Africans call a *braai* (which means roast). The secret to cooking delicious grilled meat lies in the marinade (sauce) in which you soak the meat overnight.

You will need:
1. Wooden skewers
2. Measuring cups
3. Measuring spoons
4. Knife
5. Whisk
6. Cutting board
7. Bowl
8. ½ cup (80 g) sweet chutney
9. ¼ cup (40 g) mayonnaise
10. ¼ cup (40 g) tomato sauce
11. A dash of Worcester sauce
12. 1 teaspoon mustard
13. ½ cup (120 ml) apple cider vinegar
14. ½ cup (120 ml) cooking oil
15. Small pieces of beef, pork, lamb or chicken
16. A green capsicum
17. A red capsicum

1 Whisk the chutney, mayonnaise, tomato sauce, Worcester sauce, mustard, apple cider vinegar amd cooking oil together in a bowl.

2 Have your adult helper chop the meat into small cubes. Leave them to soak in the sauce overnight—the longer the better! Then chop the green and red capsicums into bite-size pieces.

3 Use the wooden skewers to skewer a mixture of pieces of meat and capsicum.

4 Ask your adult helper to grill the *sosaties*. Delicious!

South Korea

KKAEGANGJONG

The Korean peninsula is surrounded by the Korea Strait to the south, the Sea of Japan to the east and Korea Bay and the Yellow Sea to the west.

South Koreans enjoy sweet cakes and other Korean desserts only on festive occasions. *Kkaegangjong* is a sesame seed biscuit that is eaten on festive days.

You will need:
1. Measuring cup
2. Frying pan
3. Saucepan
4. Wooden spoon
5. Measuring spoons
6. Slightly less than ¼ cup (50 g) black sesame seeds
7. Slightly less than ¼ cup (50 g) white sesame seeds
8. ¼ cup (50 g) light brown sugar
9. 8 tablespoons golden syrup

1 In the frying pan, heat the white sesame seeds. Remove the pan from the heat when the sesame seeds start to pop. When the pan has cooled, put the seeds into a bowl. Do the same for the black sesame seeds.

2 Mix the syrup and sugar in a saucepan. Heat this until the sugar has dissolved. When the mixture has cooled, mix half of this syrup into the bowl containing the black sesame seeds. Mix the other half into the bowl containing the white sesame seeds.

3 Tear off a piece of the white sesame seed paste. Shape it into a flattened, round piece as you see in the picture. When you have finished with the white sesame paste, you can start on the black! Now you have a delicious dessert!

Spain

CREMA FRITA

A narrow waterway, called the Strait of Gibraltar, separates Spain from Africa. Its closest African neighbour is Morocco. To the north, its neighbours are Andorra and France and, to the west, Portugal. The Mediterranean Sea lies to the south and east and mountain ranges are found in the north and south of the country.

Crema frita means fried custard in Spanish. It is a typical Spanish dessert. Try making this delicious treat but be sure to have an adult help you do the frying!

You will need:

1. Measuring cup
2. Saucepan
3. Measuring spoons
4. Square cake pan
5. Whisk
6. Spatula
7. Sieve
8. 2 cups (480 ml) milk
9. 1 cup (227 g) butter
10. 4 egg yolks
11. 1 teaspoon vanilla powder or extract
12. ½ cup (60 g) breadcrumbs
13. ½ cup (60 g) flour
14. 1 egg, beaten
15. 1 cup (230 g) sugar
16. Powdered sugar

1 Mix egg yolks, sugar, flour and vanilla in the saucepan.

2 Add milk and cook gently, stirring all the time until the mixture thickens into a custard.

3 Pour the custard into the cake pan and let it cool. Chill in the refrigerator until firm.

4 Cut the custard into squares and coat each square with beaten egg and breadcrumbs. Ask an adult to heat the butter in a frying pan and fry each square until it is browned. Use the sieve to sprinkle powdered sugar over each square. Serve this treat hot.

Sweden

COCONUT CHOCOLATE BALLS

Sweden is in northern Europe. Sweden's neighbours are Norway, Denmark and Finland. These are called the Nordic or Scandinavian countries. The people of Scandinavia share a similar culture, history and language.

These wonderful chocolate balls are a favourite with Swedish children. They are easy to make and they taste great! Give them away as a present or share them with a friend!

You will need:

1. Mixing bowl
2. Wooden spoon
3. Measuring cups
4. Measuring spoons
5. ½ cup (113 g) butter
6. 1 cup (240 g) sugar
7. 3 cups (360 g) oatmeal flakes
8. Coconut for rolling, grated
9. 2 tablespoons chocolate powder
10. 1 tablespoon vanilla extract
11. 1 teaspoon instant coffee granules

1 Cream butter and sugar in a large mixing bowl.

2 Add chocolate powder, coffee granules, vanilla extract and oatmeal flakes and mix.

3 Make small balls the size of table tennis balls.

4 Roll balls in grated coconut. Put them in the refrigerator to cool before serving.

Switzerland

SWISS FONDUE

Switzerland lies in the heart of Europe. It is a small country that can be crossed by car in only one day. Despite its small size, there is no shortage of natural wonders in Switzerland, with its many lakes, mountains and valleys.

Emmentaler and Gruyère are well-known Swiss cheeses and are ingredients in the famous Swiss dish, fondue, where chunks of bread are dipped into melted cheese. According to tradition, anyone who lets bread fall into the cheese has to buy drinks for the evening!

You will need:

1. Pot
2. 2 two-pronged forks
3. Measuring spoons
4. Pot holder
5. Wooden spoon
6. 1¼ cups (300 ml) apple juice
7. Chunks of white bread
8. 1 tablespoon butter
9. 1 teaspoon corn starch
10. ½ teaspoon ground nutmeg
11. 1 clove crushed garlic
12. 1 cup (250 g) grated Gruyère cheese
13. 1 cup (250 g) grated Emmentaler cheese

1 Have an adult help you melt the butter in a pot. Cook the garlic in the butter over low heat for 1 minute.

2 Mix the corn flour into the apple juice and pour the mixture into the pot.

4 Keep the pot warm with a food warmer and dip the bread into the cheese using two-pronged forks. Delicious!

3 Add the cheeses to the pot and cook over low heat for 5 minutes, stirring continuously. After the cheese has melted, add the nutmeg.

Thailand

WATERMELON SLUSHIES

The Kingdom of Thailand is in Southeast Asia. At the heart of the country is the Chao Phraya River delta, where Thai farmers grow rice and other crops in the fertile soil. It's hot all year round in Thailand.

During the hot weather, there's nothing like an icy watermelon slushie to cool you down. This recipe makes four cooling slushies.

You will need:
1. Knife
2. Wooden spoon
3. Measuring spoons
4. Blender
5. Ice cubes
6. A large slice of seedless watermelon
7. 1 tablespoon sugar or honey

1 Put the ice cubes in the blender. Ask your adult helper to mix the ice cubes until they are crushed. You may need to stop and use the spoon to help break up the ice.

2 Have your adult helper to cut the watermelon into pieces. You'll need about 2 cups of watermelon. Add the watermelon to the ice and blend for 1 minute, until the mixture is slushy.

3 Add the sugar or honey and blend for 10 seconds. Pour the slush into glasses. Now sit back, enjoy your icy slush and cool off!

Trinidad

CALLALOO

Trinidad is a beautiful island in the Caribbean that lies north of the South American country of Venezuela. It is the larger island of the nation known as Trinidad and Tobago.

Callaloo is a savoury green soup that is very popular in Trinidad. The word *callaloo* is also used to describe any mix of races, cultures or personalities. *Callaloo* is, therefore, a soup made from a mix of different kinds of green vegetables.

You will need:
1. Large saucepan
2. Cutting board
3. Measuring spoons
4. Ladle
5. Measuring cup
6. 4 cups (1 kg) spinach leaves
7. 12 ladies fingers, sliced
8. 1 green capsicum, diced
9. 3 crushed cloves garlic
10. 2 chopped chives
11. 1 chopped onion
12. 1 chicken bouillon cube
13. 1 teaspoon salt
14. 1 teaspoon pepper
15. 1 teaspoon thyme
16. 2 cups (500 ml) water

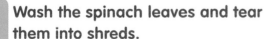

1 Wash the spinach leaves and tear them into shreds.

2 Put the water into the saucepan with all the other ingredients. Ask your adult helper to put the saucepan on the stove over low heat.

3 After the soup starts to boil, let it simmer for 30 minutes, stirring occasionally. When it begins to thicken, it is ready to eat. Add salt and pepper to taste. Ladle the *callaloo* into 2 bowls and serve it with bread and butter.

Turkey

PUMPKIN DESSERT

Turkey is a bridge between Europe and Asia. For over 600 years, the country was the heart of the Ottoman Empire that stretched across Europe, Northern Africa and Arabia. Today, Turkey is much smaller. Its famous city, Istanbul, is the only city in the world to lie on two continents.

Pumpkins are popular in Turkey. They are sold at markets and shops and can be used in both sweet and spicy recipes. This pumpkin dessert is very easy to make and is a healthy alternative to the rich, sweet baklava (BAH-klah-vah) pastries found on the menus of most Turkish restaurants.

You will need:
1. Spoon
2. Wide saucepan
3. Measuring cup
4. ½ sweet pumpkin, washed and sliced into wedges
5. 1½ cups (350 g) granulated sugar
6. ¼ cup (50 g) walnuts

1 Place the pumpkin wedges in the the saucepan. Ask an adult to put the pan carefully on a hot stove.

2 Spoon the sugar over the pumpkin wedges and pour enough water into the pan to cover the pumpkin pieces. Cover the pan and cook over medium heat until the pumpkin is tender.

3 Ask an adult to help you put the pumpkin wedges on a dish. Sprinkle the wedges with chopped walnuts and allow them to cool. Eat this sweet treat with a knife and fork.

Ukraine

STRAWBERRY KYSIL

Ukraine is one of the largest countries in Europe in terms of land and population. The Black Sea borders half of southern Ukraine. Ukraine is divided into 25 states, called *oblasts* [OB-lahsts]. The capital is Kiev. A popular dessert in Ukraine is *kysil* (kih-SIL). *Kysil* is usually eaten after lunch or dinner. It can be made with almost any kind of berry but strawberries are the best!

You will need:
1. Saucepan
2. Wooden spoon
3. Sieve
4. Mixing bowl
5. Measuring spoons
6. 2 boxes fresh strawberries, stems removed
7. 2 cups (500 ml) cold water
8. ¾ cup (180 g) sugar
9. 1 tablespoon potato flour dissolved in 1 tablespoon water

1 Place strawberries and 2 cups water in the pot. Boil the fruit on high for 1 minute. Then reduce the heat to low and allow the fruit to simmer uncovered for 10 to 15 minutes or until the fruit is tender.

2 Push the strawberries through the sieve with a wooden spoon. Collect the juice in a mixing bowl.

3 Stir in sugar. Return the fruit to the pot and boil over high heat for 2 minutes.

4 Reduce the heat to moderate and stir in the dissolved potato flour. Cook for another 2 or 3 minutes, stirring until it thickens slightly.

5 Cool to lukewarm and refrigerate for 4 hours before serving. Then enjoy a delicious treat.

United States

PUMPKIN PIE

The United States of America is the third largest country in the world. It covers about half of the North American continent, stretching from the Atlantic Ocean in the east to the Pacific Ocean in the west. Its only neighbours are Canada to the north and Mexico to the south.

A Thanksgiving meal would not be complete without pumpkin pie—a simple, delicious treat you and an adult helper can make and enjoy!

You will need:
1. Blender
2. Measuring cup
3. Pot holder
4. Butter knife
5. Measuring spoons
6. 2 cups (450 g) mashed or canned pumpkin
7. Whipped cream
8. ⅔ cup (150 g) brown sugar
9. 2 eggs
10. A prepared piecrust
11. ½ teaspoon ground nutmeg
12. ¼ teaspoon ground allspice
13. 1 teaspoon ground cinnamon
14. ½ teaspoon ground ginger
15. ½ cup (120 ml) milk

1 Have an adult help you preheat the oven to 180°C (350°F). Put the pumpkin in a blender with the eggs, milk, brown sugar and spices. Blend the mixture until it is smooth.

2 Pour the pumpkin mixture into the piecrust.

3 Ask an adult to help you put the pie in the oven. Bake the pie for 40 to 45 minutes. To test if it is ready, stick a butter knife in the pie. The knife should come out clean.

4 Let the pie cool. Then top it with whipped cream, cut it into slices and serve it to your friends!

Vietnam

STICKY RICE WITH MANGO

Vietnam is a long, narrow country shaped something like an "S". It lies in the centre of East Asia. About three-quarters of the land is covered with mountains. The other quarter has been cut into terraced rice fields.

Sticky rice is a common food you'll see at many Vietnamese festivals. Here's a great recipe for a light, refreshing dish that is delicious anytime.

You will need:

1. Cutting board
2. Measuring cups
3. Measuring spoons
4. Wooden spoon
5. Sieve
6. Knife
7. Double boiler
8. 1 cup (225 g) glutinous rice
9. Water
10. 2 mangoes
11. ½ cup (120 ml) coconut cream
12. ½ teaspoon salt
13. ¼ cup (60 g) sugar

1 Soak the rice in water for 2 hours. Drain well.

2 In a double boiler, bring water to a boil and steam rice for 30 minutes.

3 Slice the mangoes lengthwise and remove the seeds.

4 Mix the coconut cream, salt and sugar into the rice.

5 Place rice on a plate and arrange mango slices around it.

INDEX

A

allspice 42, 98
almonds 70, 71
Anzac Biscuits 8
apple 32, 33
apple cider vinegar 80, 81
apple juice 32, 88, 89
avocado 56, 57

B

baking powder 12, 22, 23, 34, 42, 43,
    44, 45, 46, 47
baking soda 8, 9, 12, 66, 67
banana 6, 14, 15, 54, 55, 66, 68
Banch 58
beef 58, 59
Besitos de Coco 72
Blancmange 36
Bramborak 20
breadcrumbs 84, 85
Buche de Noel 30
Burfi 38
buttermilk 12, 13

C

cabbage 58, 59
Callaloo 92
capsicum 80, 81, 92
cardamom 28, 29, 32, 52, 53
cashew nuts 38, 39
cayenne pepper 26, 27
chicken bouillon cube 92
chives 92
chocolate chips 44, 45
cinnamon 22, 23, 26, 27, 32, 42, 74, 75,
    76, 77, 98
cloves 10, 26, 27, 32, 42, 92
Cocada Branca 10
cocoa powder 60
coconut 10, 11, 36, 37, 52, 53, 54, 55,
    68, 72, 86, 87, 100, 101
Coconut Chocolate Balls 86
coconut cream 36, 37, 100, 101

coconut milk 52, 53
coriander 40, 41
coriander leaves 56, 57
corn 68
corn syrup 8, 9
cream 48, 49
cream cheese 74, 75
Crema Frita 84

D

Dabo Kolo 26
dried apricots 76
dried figs 76
dried prunes 76

E

Emmentaler cheese 88
Ensalada de Frutas 18
evaporated milk 36, 37, 66, 67, 68

F

fenugreek 22, 23
Fried *Tempeh* 40
frozen custard 68, 69

G

garlic 88, 89, 92, 93
gelatin 36, 37
ginger 26, 27, 64, 65, 98, 99
Ginger Beer 64
glutinous rice 100, 101
golden syrup 82, 83
Grandma's Nut Cake 22
Gruyere cheese 88
Guacamole 56

H

Halo Halo 68
Hamantaschen 44
honey 42, 43, 90, 91

I

instant coffee 86, 87

instant dried yeast 52, 53

J

jalapeno pepper 56, 57
jello powder 18, 19

K

Khoshaf 76
Kindergluwein 32
kiwifruit 18, 19, 62, 63
Kiwi-Mango Sorbet 62
Kkaegangjong 82
Koulourakia 34

L

ladies fingers 92, 93
Leche con Platano 14
lemon juice 32, 33, 56, 57
light soy sauce 40, 41

M

macadamia nut 68
majoram 20
mango 62, 63, 100, 101
maple syrup 12, 13
mayonnaise 80, 81
Milkshake 54
mozzarella cheese 46
mushrooms 46,
mustard 80, 81

N

Natilla 66
Nut *Mazurek* 70
nutmeg 42, 43, 76, 77, 88, 89, 98, 99

O

oatmeal flakes 86, 87
olives 46
Onigiri 50
onion 46, 56, 57, 58, 59, 92, 93
orange juice 62, 63,
oregano 46

P

palm fruit 68
Pancakes with Maple Syrup 12
parmesan cheese 46
peach 6, 7
Peach *Licuado* 6
pineapple 18, 19, 48, 49
Pineapple Fool 48
Pizza 46
potato flour 96, 97
potatoes 42, 43
pumpkin 94, 95, 98, 99
Pumpkin Dessert 94
Pumpkin Pie 98

R

rolled oats 8, 9
rice 50, 51
Rice Pancakes 52
Russian Sweet Treats 74
raisins 76, 77
rice flour 16, 17, 52, ,53, 78, 79

S

Scones 24
Scottish Shortbread 78
seaweed 50, 51
self-raising flour 24, 25
seltzer water 64, 65
Shamrock Cookies 42
Shrove Tuesday Buns 28
Sosaties 80
sour plums 50, 51
spinach leaves 92, 93
Sticky Rice with Mango 100
strawberry 18, 19, 54, 55, 96, 97
Strawberry Kysil 96
Sugar Hearts 60
sweet chutney 80, 81
sweet potato 68, 69
sweetened condensed milk 36, 37, 38, 39
sweetened kidney beans 68

Swiss Fondue 88

T

Tang Yuan 16
tapioca 68
tempeh 40, 41
thyme 92, 93
tomato 56, 57
tomato sauce 46, 47, 80, 81

V

vanilla extract 34, 34, 44, 45, 48, 49, 54, 55, 72, 73, 84, 85, 86, 87
vegetable oil 52, 53

W

walnuts 74, 75, 94, 95
watermelon 90, 91
Watermelon Slushies 90
wheat flour 26, 27
white sesame seeds 34, 35, 50, 51, 82, 83
worchester sauce 80, 81

Y

yoghurt 76, 77